# Introduction

The word fragile is defined as meaning dainty, delicate, fine or flimsy but can also suggest weakness or frailty. Some of the samples illustrated are beautifully delicate and lacy yet their structures are fairly strong. Other works show a wonderful fragility but these are not durable enough to withstand heavy handling. However, these could be included as part of or within other textiles. They could hang as an exhibit or be for a special purpose where care and preservation are the considerations. Less conventional methods and materials have been used and we are aware that melting and fusing plastics are covered in other publications.

It is hoped that some of the ideas and experiments shown within the following pages will encourage readers to take a fresh look at the many ways of creating fragile fabrics that exhibit innovative qualities and can provide an exciting challenge.

**Sheer Fabrics**
Natural fibres such as chiffon, tulle, fine silk and organdy are just a few beautiful materials to seduce textile artists, dress designers and other creative practitioners. A wondrous range of sheer, synthetic fabrics are also readily available. Some are novelty materials featuring sparkling yarns and sequins or are printed in a myriad of colours. All these fabrics are extremely delicate and present very special qualities but they can be difficult to handle due to their flimsiness. However it is very worthwhile persevering as superb effects are achievable. Those that are transparent can be overlaid one on another to create further colourings, provide subtle hues or partially hide images set between. Diaphanous white may represent innocence or be protective. Soft, pale coloured sheers suggest passive, serene and even secretive qualities. By contrast, brightly coloured sheers can be exciting, exotic and seductive whereas darker hues may hint at hidden depths, menace and intrigue.

Hand stitching with fine threads will gently interrupt and enhance the surface. Heavier stitching may distort the cloth unless it is applied to a firmer ground fabric.

Some synthetics even when washed do not possess the softness and draping qualities that natural fibres exhibit. This may be a limiting factor depending on the project or item visualised. They can also appear to contain a 'diva' element and can overwhelm a design so caution is advised. They may have a strong 'personality', feature too much and not settle well alongside other natural sheers. An advantage is the materials are generally much cheaper to buy and a disadvantage of not hanging as softly as natural materials.

***Above:*** *This sample shows squares of synthetic sheer fabrics that were cut out with a soldering tool in order to prevent fraying. Having been positioned between layers of soluble film, all sections were joined together with French knots.*

***Below:*** *Running stitches in a fine silk joined all the slithers of sheer fabrics together having been sandwiched as described above. Straight stitches decorated some of the design. It would have been extremely difficult to work these samples without using this technique. The flimsy characteristics would have made the project very frustrating.*

***Cover:*** *Hydrangea petal cloth,* *see page 22.*

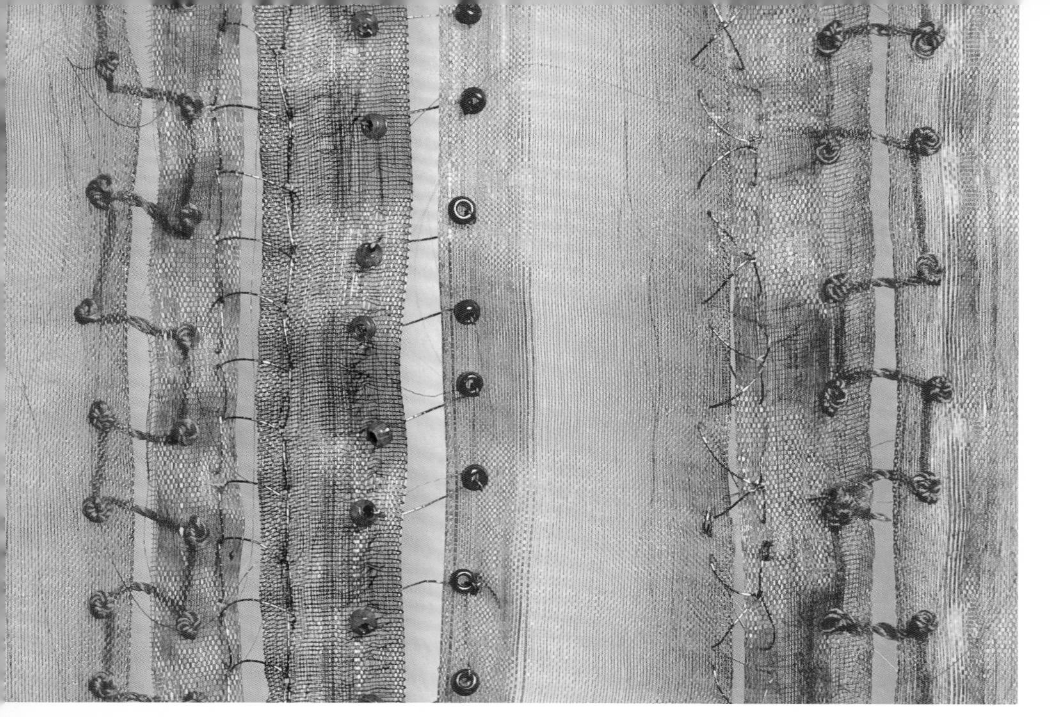

A variety of soluble films can provide support for working with the most fragile of fabrics making it possible to create delicate, innovative work. Spend time experimenting with an assortment of sheers to learn how to handle them.
It is hoped that the following questions and answers may be helpful.

**Q: How can I make a delicate lacy network using sheer fabrics, many of which are so difficult to handle?**

A: Bondaweb or fusible webbing can be carefully ironed to the back of the fabric and the protective paper will enable shapes to be cut more easily as well as limiting the fraying. Take care to monitor the heat of the iron. It needs to be hot enough to activate the glue but not so hot as to melt, shrink or distort the cloth. Shapes can be cut out, the protective paper peeled away and the patterned pieces placed onto another semi opaque material. These can then be ironed in place, again using the correct heat setting on the iron. Baking parchment should be used both on top and beneath to protect the fabric, iron and the ironing board. (see Book 3, Bonding & Beyond)

If open spaces or a lacy design is planned, 'Aquabond' or similar is an extremely useful soluble film which allows an open work design of fabric and threads to be placed directly on the sticky surface. When satisfied with the final arrangement, a thin transparent soluble film such as 'Guilletta' is positioned on top to trap all threads or fabrics in place. Machine stitching can then be worked to build up the design and link all areas one to another. Alternatively, sheers can be bonded onto 'Solusheet', a non sticky soluble stabiliser, which would eliminate the need for a top soluble film but the finished work may result in a stiffish finish and not so soft to handle. A finer fusing material such as 'Misty Fuse' may help to lessen this aspect.

**Q: Having succeeded in joining all sections together using a fine, colour toning thread, how can the lines of stitching be less obvious?**

A: A much paler tone of colour or invisible thread may well achieve a more subtle result.

**Q: What precautions can be taken if an symmetrical pattern is required?**

A: The basic shapes bonded or placed in position should all be the same size and placed accurately. This action will enable any hand or machine stitching to be worked evenly. A boldly marked plan placed beneath the sheer cloth or a soluble film can act as a guide.

**Q: How can I limit the fraying?**

A: Before purchasing a range of sheer fabrics, look at the cut edge on the roll (bale) to see whether the cloth frays readily. Most sheers do but some more than others. If the fabric is synthetic, shapes can be cut out with a fine nibbed heat tool as the heat will seal the edge. Always stretch the material tautly in a frame and observe health and safety rules by wearing a protective mask so as not to inhale toxic fumes. The edges of fabric pieces cut with scissors can be sealed to deter fraying by gently running a heated soldering iron along the edges. Plan to make more shapes than needed as it is usual that some will be singed more than others during this process. As already mentioned bonding shapes to a background inhibits fraying. Machined straight or zig-zag stitches, fine hand stitches such as cross, herring bone or buttonhole could all help to lessen further fraying. It may be appropriate to iron tiny turnings if dealing with fine silks and cottons before being stitched in place.

Remember to trim all ends of machine and hand threads from the back of the piece as your work progresses. It is very disappointing to see lots of tangled ends showing through and even more so after the film is washed away.

Points to consider when dealing with invisible thread-

- It can be really tricky to use. It seems to have a life of its own. Although time consuming and at times frustrating it can provide just the right effect for certain projects.
- Placing a dark material or paper behind the needle will help to thread invisible thread more easily.
- Sewing around to link fabric shapes trapped between two soluble films can sometimes be taxing as the invisible thread is difficult to see alongside the shiny top layer and can hinder and slow down the stitching action.

**Left:** *Strips of sheer materials, some with selvedges, others with turned edges were decoratively joined together with French knots, cross and chain stitches to form a fragile cloth.*

**Right:** *Several sheer materials were backed with 'Bondaweb' to ease the task of cutting out decorative motifs. The supporting backing paper was peeled away and the shape placed on sticky soluble and covered with the transparent film. Invisable thread was machined from one shape to another to link all elements of the design. Free motion machine stitching and hand stitching in fine silks decorated all parts before the supporting cloth was washed away. The shapes could have been bonded on the non sticky, 'Solusheet' , stretched taut in a frame and then stitched as required. The former method is a little more stable and is firm enough to machine stitch without a frame and yet remains pliable enough to suit hand stitching.*

**Below:** *This arrangement shows the various stages of the bonding method where the sheers have 'Bondaweb' ironed on the back of delicate fabrics, shapes drawn and cut away ready for final application as described. In the background, very fine polyester chiffon with applied shapes and stitching is shown supported by a soluble stabiliser ensuring much easier handling throughout the creative process.*

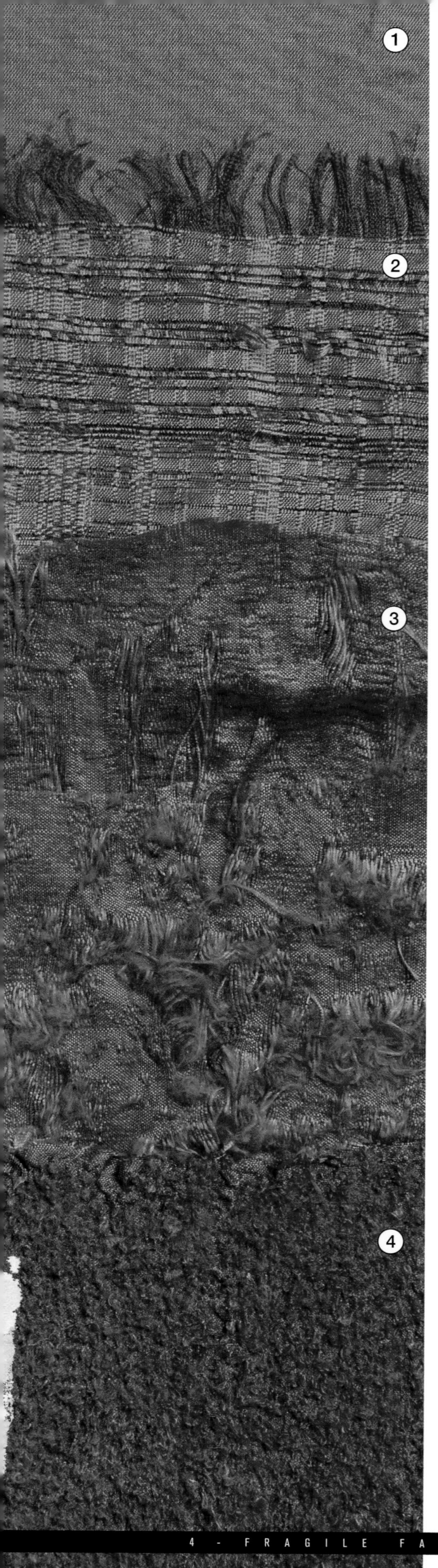


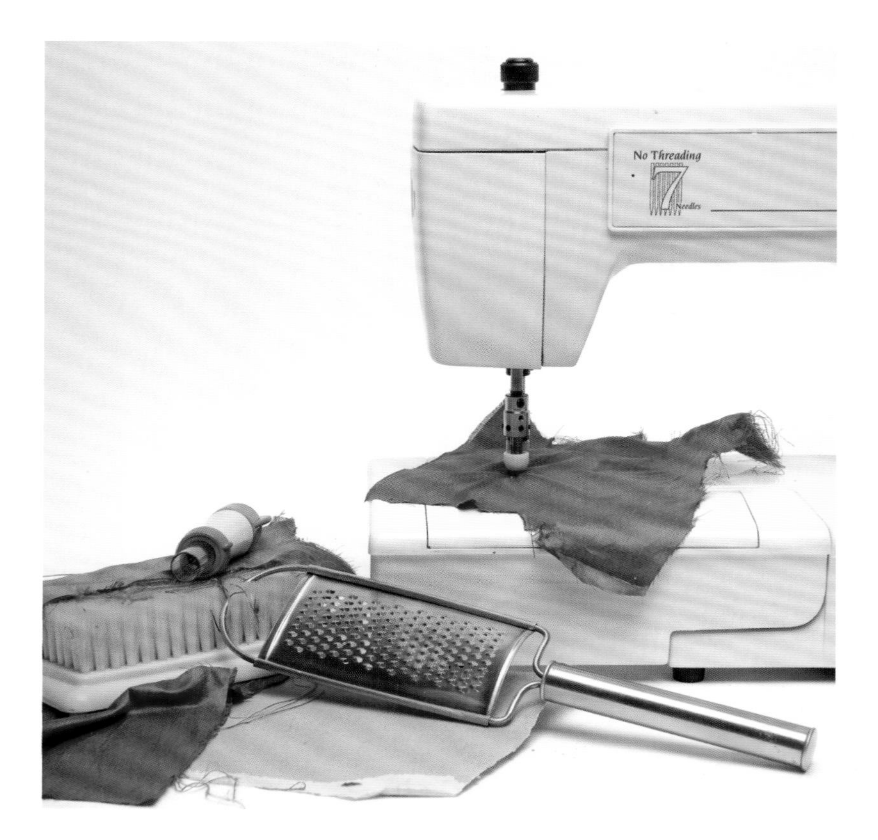


# Deconstruction & Disintegration

Old fabrics in museums will often feature signs of age and distress although great efforts are made to preserve and prevent them from further decay. Weighted silk, a technique used in the eighteenth and early nineteenth century will inevitably decay and in many ways that adds to its sense of the past. Tiny scraps of fabric from tombs have a poignancy that adds to their very human appeal.

We can use these marks and surfaces to add contextual clues to our own work where appropriate.

Fabrics may be altered in many ways depending on the fibre and method of manufacture. Removing threads from woven fabrics will give the appearance of fragility whilst inevitably weakening the fabric.
Felt can be teased apart in several ways to make a gossamer like cloth.

Synthetics respond to heat and the use of soldering and heat tools will create many diverse effects (always remember to wear masks and work in a well ventilated room or outside). Fabrics decay naturally by bacterial degradation, friction, water damage, and exposure to extremes of weather.

It can be useful to mimic these effects by placing fabric in running water or ponds, burying it in earth or exposing it to the elements to achieve some subtle markings although this will take time.

Useful tools and materials for altering and distressing surfaces include sandpaper, files, cheese graters, rocks and stones, dry felting needles and an embellishing (needle punch) machine. These can be used in varying degrees to produce subtle or dramatic effects as desired.

***Illustrations far left:*** *A piece of shot silk has been modified in various ways to achieve a variety of textures.*

*1. Warp and weft threads withdrawn*

*2. Fabric distressed between a cheese grater and a rock*

*3. Hand felting needles can be used to good effect*

*4. An embellishing machine creates dramatic surfaces at speed*

***Above:*** *Snowdrift - An unusually heavy fall of snow turned the garden into a fragile impermanent wilderness that slowly melted away revealing lacelike drifts. The challenge was to create these delicate and ephemeral qualities in fabric and thread.*

*An embellishing machine was used to distress synthetic lace and wool viscose felt until it barely held together. 'Aquabond' soluble was used to stabilize this very delicate background so that it could be worked. 'Drifts' of distressed lace and silk fibres were placed over the soluble ground with 'Guilletta' over the top. In this way the fragile sandwich could be stitched with ease. Great care was taken when dissolving it in warm water so that it would not disintegrate.*

*When dry, more embellishing with the machine further distorted the fabric into gentle dimensional folds.*

***Right:*** *The wool viscose felt was dyed with tea and during storage moths became trapped in the bag and reduced it to a fine holey fabric.*

*The next layer down is the same wool viscose felt, undyed but worked to a fine gossamer with an embellishing machine.*

*Similarly synthetic lace has been distressed with an embellishing machine.*

# Distorting Sheers

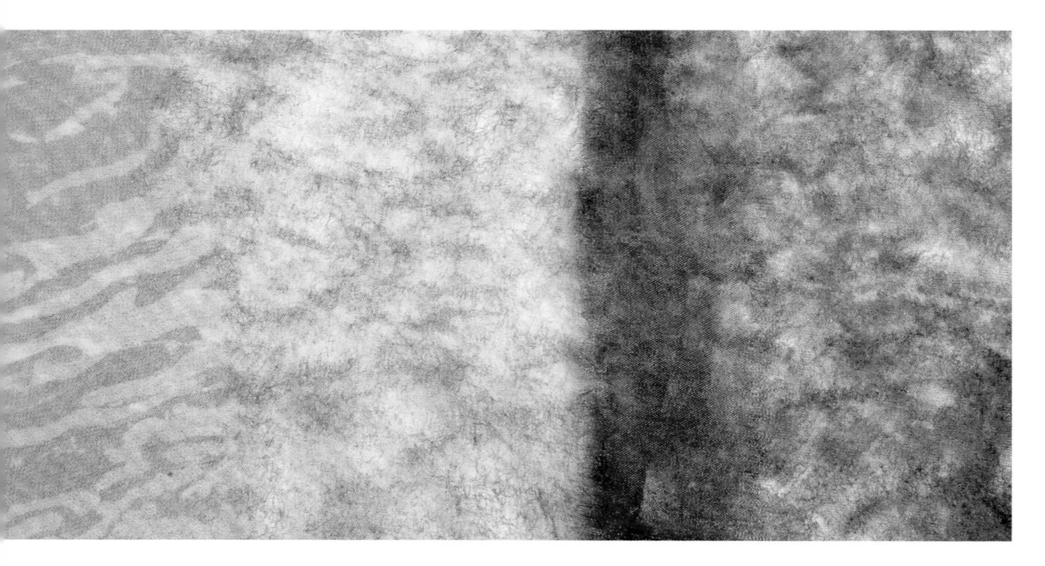

Interesting effects can be achieved on a wide variety of sheers by gentle distortion. Synthetics and natural fibres will react differently depending on their composition.

On this page a white silk chiffon was screen printed through a 'thermofax' (see pages 22/23) with water patterns. It was further developed by discharging colour from the print through the same 'thermofax'.

The patterning was the first stage but to gain a more atmospheric and abstract effect further work was required. The image was gently distorted with an embellishing machine that teased the threads apart but didn't destroy them. When working in this way it is best to hold the fabric quite taut or use a frame to prevent excessive puckering. This rendered the fabric very fragile and to complete it, the work was applied to a bronze coloured lamé (see left) to give the shimmering water patterns. At this stage further stitching by hand or machine could be added.

There are many synthetic sheers available and in innumerable colours but the quality of surface is not always sympathetic to textile interpretations. They may be cut and distorted with heated stencil cutters and heat tools and successfully coloured with transfer dyes. However the embellishing machine can offer the possibility of totally transforming synthetics.

On the opposite page a range of coloured synthetics have been used to create a colourful carpet. To begin, two contrasting colours were embellished together and combined to create another colour way. This was repeated several times with different colours.

Having assembled a number of shapes constructed in this method, they were cut and embellished in different combinations several times before the final arrangement. In places there are two or three overlays creating even more colours. Varying shapes were assembled and then joined with the machine to form even more interesting hues. The whole piece has been created in this way.

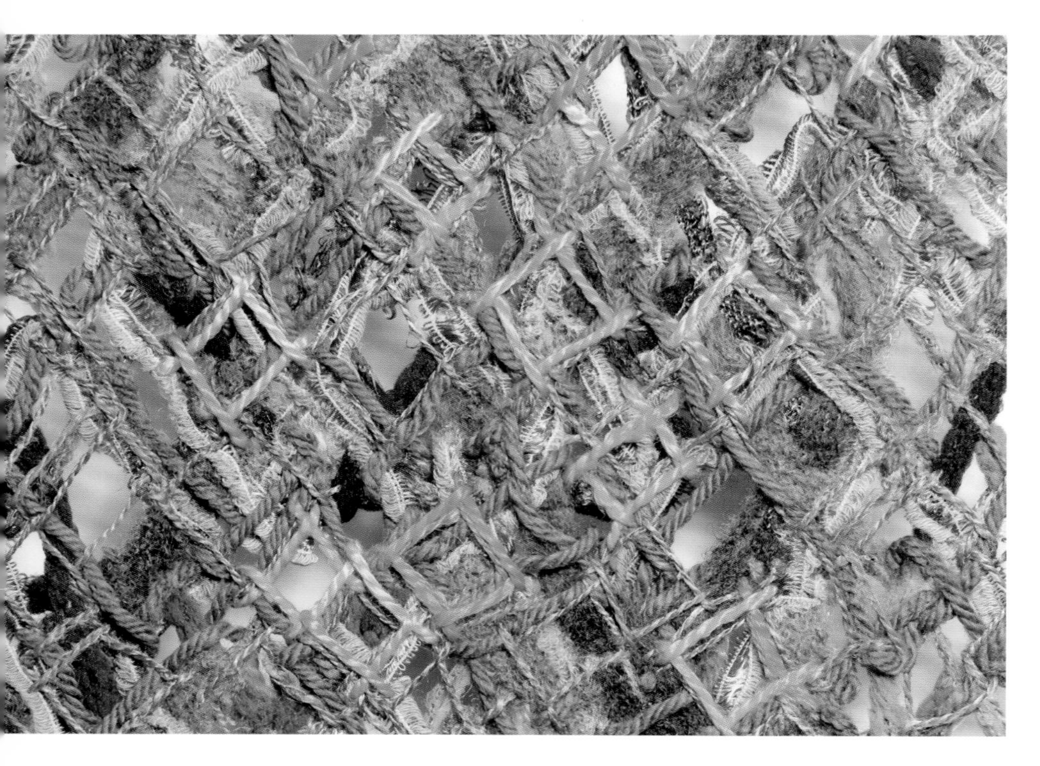

# Hand stitching on soluble film to make a fragile lace

Over the years, a few soluble materials have been suitable for hand stitching allowing a range of yarns to be sewn without the base 'fabric' (film) splitting. Most have caused great frustration and alienated many embroiderers.

Earlier books have suggested machining a grid or mesh of straight stitches to provide a base for hand stitches to be worked into, enabling the construction of a lacy pattern. This approach is still a functional method to use.

The boiling water fabric which looked similar to organdy was excellent for this process but sadly some specialist silks and rayons lost some of their colour and lustre when plunged into boiling water in order to wash away the base fabric. As many embroiderers dye their own threads and are seduced by the wonderfully coloured yarns that are so tempting and can be found in specialist shops or at the shows, using this particular method is not suitable.
The white 'Solusheet' or 'Solufleece' is a better material to use as it is stronger and washes away easily when placed in tepid water.

The combination of machine and hand stitching can be most effective. The machine stitches can provide a 'safety net' to ensure all sections of the cloth hold together but also can slightly stiffen the cloth effecting the overall feel.

More experiments have been made to create cloths entirely in hand stitches so that some embroiderers can create fragile fabrics without having to be adept with the machine.
When constructing a fabric using soluble materials, it must be remembered that all parts of the design must link whether it be with a stitch, some fabric, a thread or a bead.

Creating a lacy pattern just with hand stitches can present an intriguing challenge and one or two of the first samples partially disintegrated during the dissolving process.

One stitch was selected to work all over the allotted area in a range of medium to thick yarns overlapping them at the outset. To commence, the threads were fastened on by a knot at the edge outside of the design. When all work is completed, the knots can be cut away and the ends darned in carefully so as not to cross any lacy holes that have been created. A preferable choice may be to tie down any loose ends with a finer thread or perhaps one that has been chosen for attaching beads.

Incorporating or catching into a stitch already formed, or by piercing a thread of another will help to link. Interweaving, wrapping, knotting previously worked areas can be part of the action before continuing on to form new ones.

If a little unsure, thin strips of very fine nets or sheers can be placed on the background as a 'safety net' before commencing any stitchery. They should not necessarily feature and tones and colours should be selected to blend. Tearing or roughly cutting these pieces will help the process of integration.
Sometimes a crisply cut edge can be too noticeable.

Additional effects and security actions.
• Add beads with a finer thread.
• Machining into the stitching to secure but aim to echo the main characteristics of the base stitch so that interesting surfaces can be achieved.
• The embellishing machine can be a marvellous tool to partially fuse some areas so ensuring the stability of the piece. Always undertake this task before any beading in order not to break the needles.

***Left:*** *Cross stitches in variety of interesting thick, thin and slubbed yarns were overlapped in part on 'Solusheet', a white non sticky soluble fabric. Several threads within the sample were fused to others using the embellishing machine.*

***Right:*** *The heavier cellular shapes shown on the top section were initially backstitched on to 'Solusheet' to form the pattern before knotted buttonhole stitch and beads were embroidered on top and through the originals stitches ensuring that all areas were linked one with another. The lower section was drawn with free motion machine stitching and tiny beads were hand sewn to the lines. This process is more easily carried out before the soluble is washed away.*

***Below Left:*** *Novelty knitting yarns, silks, wools and cottons were selected to embroider dozens of French knots on 'Solusheet' taking care to link, merge and overlap in order to construct a fabric of sorts. It did disintegrate in part during the dissolving process but much was learnt from the experiment. It achieved a unique look and on reflection offered several ways of proceeding further. By keeping all samples in a notebook, fresh thoughts at a later stage could well lead to more innovative work.*

***Below Right:*** *Clusters of French knots were stitched in a range of fibres to form a grid pattern. Rows of backstitch in a medium sized silk yarn were sewn around the main sections of knots and an embellishing machine fused them to secure the piece.*

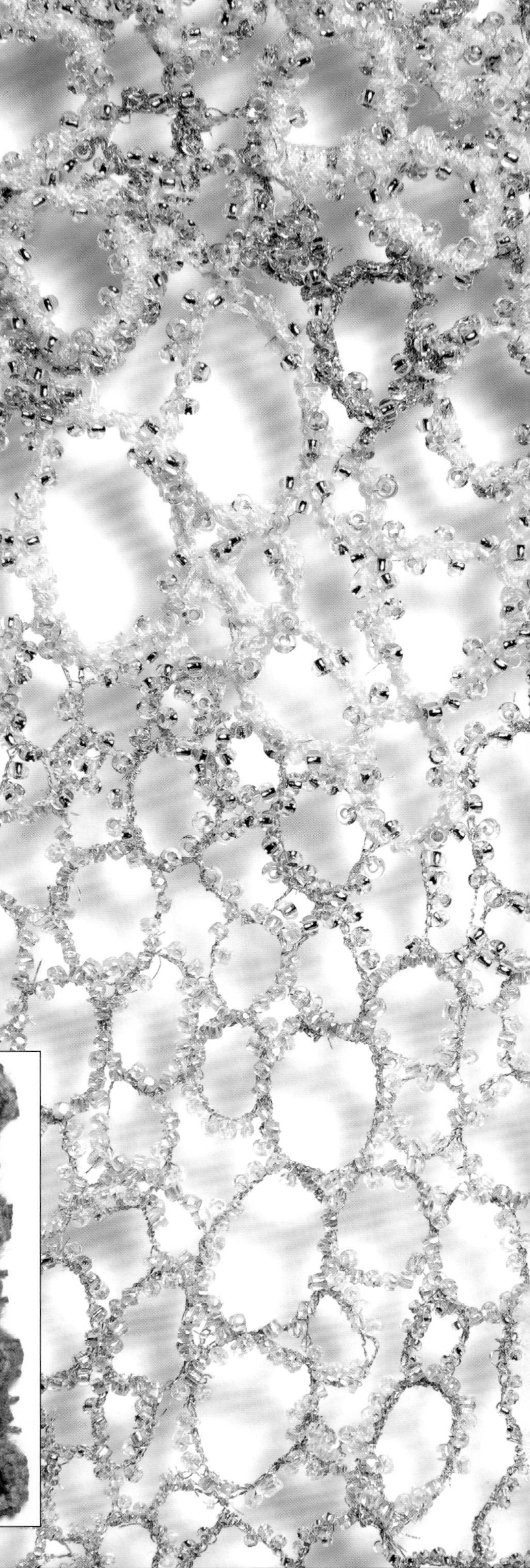

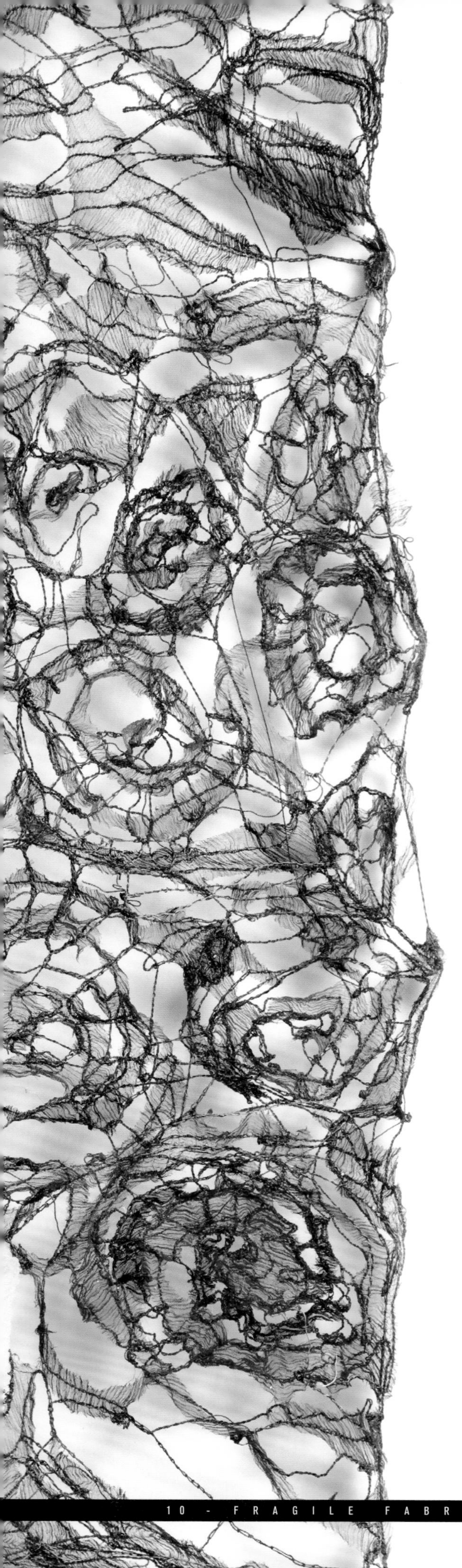

# Fossil Fragments

Two interpretations of fossil fragments are featured on these pages.

Soluble support fabrics such as the sticky 'Aquabond' or non sticky products have made the construction of fragile grids much easier.

'Aquabond' was used as the background for assembling the silk chiffon fossil and rock strata shapes featured on the left. When placed they were sandwiched under a layer of transparent 'Guilletta'. This made some otherwise unstable fabrics very manageable. The layered pieces were firm enough for machine embroidery without a hoop. The stitching needed to link all the elements and it took planning to work the stitching in a way that held the fragile structure together and yet maintained the movement of the composition.

Sometimes the unplanned holes are not evident until it has been dissolved in water. If there are gaps then they can be worked by spot patching with 'Aquabond' and 'Guilletta' before further dissolving.

The more the fabric is rinsed the softer it becomes but there are times when a little stiffness helps with the presentation of the finished piece so this can be considered at the dissolving stage. When presenting this piece the cast shadows were an important factor so the fixing held it away from the surface.

The second fragment was worked on a fine cotton died scrim. The fabric was first bonded with velvet fossil shapes before being stretched taut in a frame. In this case the frame was preferable to the sticky 'Aquabond' as distortion of the threads to produce a pulled effect needs tension and cannot take place when the fabric is fixed. Toning machine threads and free machine embroidery set to first stage zig zag, pulled and distorted the structure of the fabric. The stitching needed was worked to echo the shapes of the fossils and structures.

Once the stitching had created the lacy fabric, bugle beads were added to give the mineral glitter often found within the fossil structures.

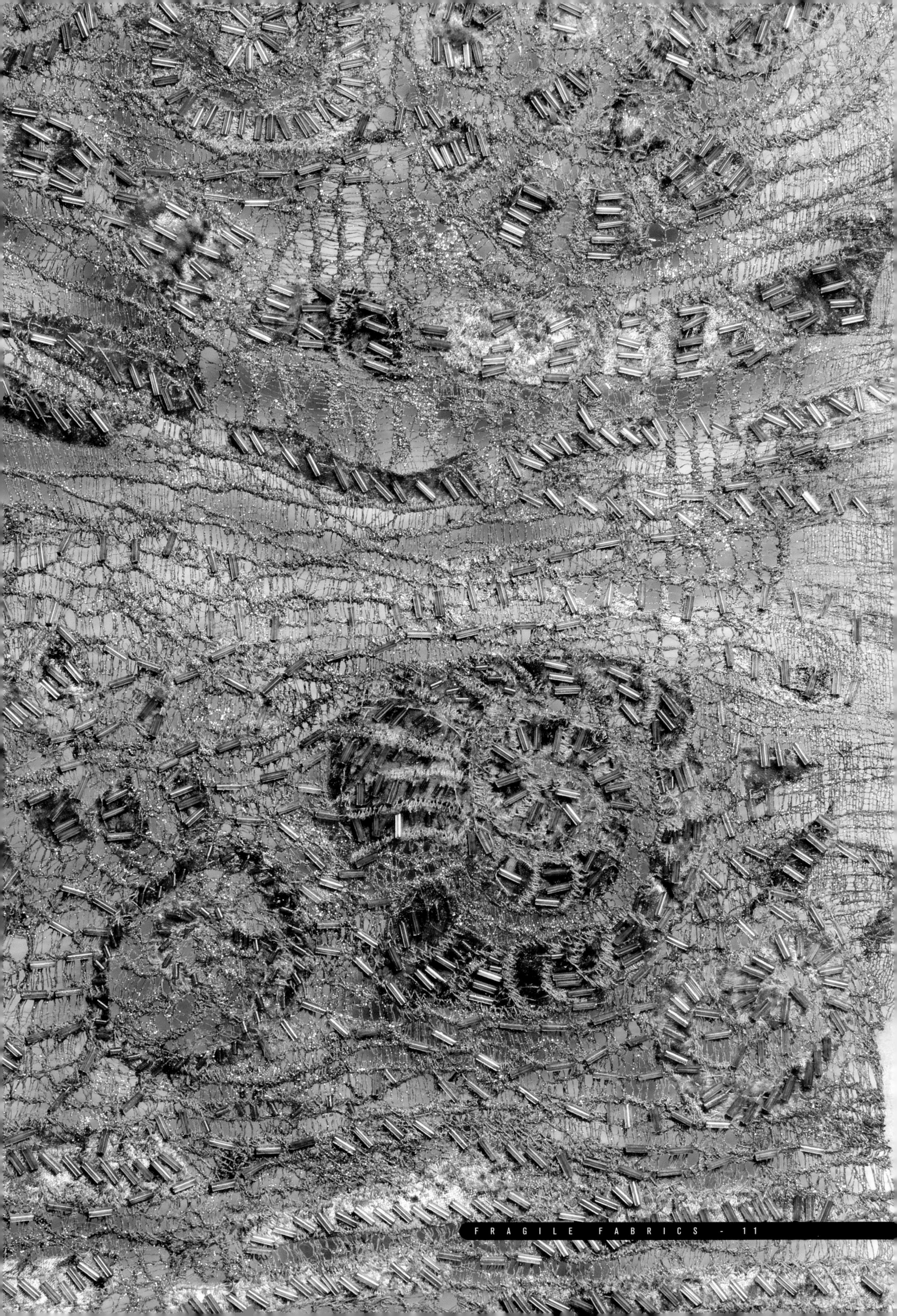

*Wild flowers inspired this sample. Textured yarns and fabric scraps were placed on 'Aquabond' and topped with 'Guilletta'. Free motion machine stitches added more drawing lines as well as linking all the shapes set down. Small flowers were created on 'Solusheet' and applied to the main piece after the soluble stabilisers have been washed away.*

# Hydrangea Fabrics

Hydrangeas have voluptuous multi-headed blooms that look lovely when in full flower and fragile when dried out.
They could provide endless sources of inspiration but in this case, the veining on an individual petal has been used as a design for screen printing.

There are many methods of screen printing but 'thermofaxes' have given opportunities for some professional and accurate printing effects in the home and they have many applications.

The black and white line drawing featured is derived from a petal. It has then been photocopied and reduced in size to be made into a 'thermofax' (see above left). This simple screen was generated from the black and white drawing.

Screens are easily available from various suppliers (see back page and list of suppliers on the web site). They can be made in sizes up to A3.
Once you have the screen it can be used in various ways to produce imagery.

Featured in the picture (above left) is a black cotton discharge fabric, (prepared for colour removal) that has been patterned by using discharge paste through the screen. Providing the screen is cleaned properly it should last a long time and be used to add colour with various printing inks or remove colour as desired.

For the detail (above right and front cover) a sheer black chiffon was discharged using discharge paste through the 'thermofax' screen to create the subtle leaf print.

Once the paste dried on the fabric a steam iron completed the discharge process (this is very smelly and should be worked outside or with a mask).
Following ironing, the fabric should be washed and in this case the fabric was then stretched out and when wet a gentle wash of silk paints flooded in.

The final stage in creating this fragile cloth was some delicate hand stitching with fine silver threads and ends knotted but uncut to give gentle movement to the work.

The piece featured on the right was screen printed using the same 'thermofax' pattern but chiefly as a guide for the stitching. The design could be drawn or printed in other ways.

The background fabric is 'Lutradur,'a synthetic material that responds to heat. Both sides of the fabric were painted with acrylic paints before overprinting the skeletal petal pattern using silver screen printing ink.
The machine stitching was worked with a cotton thread and echoed the decaying patterns.

Once completed the stitched piece was pinned to a wooden frame and a heat tool used to 'eat away' at the pattern to achieve an abstracted fragile fabric based on the hydrangea forms. Because the thread was cotton it resisted the heat and added more effectively to the skeletal structure.

It can be desirable to support fragile fabrics in order to give them body whilst maintaining their delicacy. Glues and resins are useful but sometimes become so stiff that the work can lose its textile quality,
A combination of PVA glue, cellulose paste and water can provide the stability and not overwhelm the fabric properties if used in the right proportions.

This is often a case of trial and error but one tablespoon of PVA to a pint of water and two teaspoons of cellulose paste can be a good starting point. Mix the PVA and water together first and add the cellulose paste a little at a time stirring constantly to prevent lumps from forming. The best cellulose to use does not contain anti fungicidal so it will only last for two weeks or so once mixed. Should a more robust solution be required then add more PVA or less water.

A plastic bag or bin liner can be used as a support. For the dimensional piece (right) all the pieces were painted with PVA solution. Tissue paper, scrim and net shapes were overlayed on the plastic ground to form a delicate structure of petals. When dry and peeled from its background the semitransparent fabric can be held against the light to reveal the subtle colour combinations.

To achieve the dimensional effects, sheets of tissue paper, nets and scrims were supported on plastic, then painted with the glue solution and allowed to dry. It was then possible to peel and cut them into petal shapes and stitch to the background. The glue gave them sufficient strength to hold their shape. Even though the tissue paper and scrim are fragile, the glue solution allows the petals to be stitched.

The other hydrangea fabric (above) comprises many scrim petals cut from the stiffened fabric and knitted into a fine structure using fishing wire as the base thread. (See Book 14, Connections)

Throughout the book we have looked at methods of constructing fragile fabrics that are the starting points for endless variations and are capable of adapting to a range of materials.
The techniques are there to support the ideas and the first step could be to look at fragility around you, organic decay, water patterns, reflections, images seen through a microscope, or spiders webs could be just the start.

With colours, textures and patterns to look at, the techniques and materials explored in this book can take on a much more personal dynamic and become yours.